Shade and Solace

In the shade, I found a seat,
A comfy spot with nature's heat.
The squirrels giggle and they tease,
As I nap beneath the swaying trees.

A bird does sing, but hits a wrong note,
While I munch on my peanut butter tote.
If laughter grows like ivy on bark,
I'll wake up soon, just to make my mark.

A Journey Through Green Halls

Walking through these leafy doors,
I trip on roots and tumble on floors.
The crickets chirp a comic tune,
While I dance with shadows, quite out of sync.

Each step a giggle, a slip, a fall,
In this green hall, I trip and sprawl.
With laughter echoing through the trees,
Nature's giggles bring me to my knees.

The Quiet Whisper of Leaves

The leaves confide secrets soft and low,
About slugs in ties and squirrels in tow.
"Moms, don't forget," the forest exclaims,
"The leaves are for laughing, not just for games!"

Whispers of wind make jokes take flight,
As I join the chat, feeling just right.
With a chuckle, a snicker, under blue skies,
I stroll with the humor that nature supplies.

Enigma of the Forest Floor

Oh, the forest floor is a puzzling sight,
With mushrooms in hats and bugs that take flight.
A snail in a hurry, what's that all about?
Life's little mysteries make me laugh out loud!

I tiptoe past grass, oh so deep,
Finding treasures in roots, yes, they [almost] creep!
As the sun beams down in a playful glow,
I join in the dance of the earth below.

Gatherings of Ancient Green

In the forest's snug embrace,
Fungi throw a wild soiree.
The trees sway in their leafy dance,
As squirrels plot a merry prance.

Toadstools wear their dapper hats,
While critters gossip about the rats.
In corners, shadows twist and leap,
As all join in, their secrets keep.

Old wisdom spins from bough to root,
Where silly whispers find their loot.
A game of hide-and-seek ensues,
With giggles hidden from our views.

So raise a cup to nature's jest,
Where every creature brings its best.
In laughter's shade the fun will swell,
In ancient green, all's well, all's well!

Lurking in the Verdant Shadows

Beneath the fronds in darkest gloom,
A rabbit's thrown a party boom.
With carrots, cake, and leafy cheer,
The laughter echoes far and near.

A hedgehog juggles acorn balls,
While fireflies dance down the halls.
Each bough whispers a secret tune,
As night takes charge, and bears the moon.

Jaded raccoons in their masks peek,
Stir up mischief, and play hide and seek.
The crickets chirp their choppy song,
To serenade the joy that's strong.

So let us join in this wild game,
In verdant shadows, none are tame.
With chuckles bright, the night's our stage,
As nature flips a funny page.

Hidden Letters in the Leaves

Beneath the canopy so thick,
Lies a note from a playful trick.
The wind whispers, 'Come and see!'
What secrets flutter on the tree.

Each leaf a word, a tale untold,
Of mischief wrought by sprightly bold.
A squirrel scrawls, a chipmunk draws,
Their letters grand with gnarly claws.

The message reads, 'Let's tease the dawn!'
With jests that greet the rosy lawn.
And gather near the bubbling brook,
For tales as ripe as storybooks.

So underneath this leafy roof,
The laughter spins around aloof.
In hidden letters, mirth we crave,
Nature's pen, a path to brave!

Ferns and Faeries

In the glen where ferns parade,
Faeries dance, their pranks displayed.
With emerald gowns that swirl and twirl,
They whirl about, a mischievous swirl.

They tickle toes of sleeping snails,
And whisper jokes to barnacle tails.
With laughter, light as morning dew,
Their giggles make the shy to coo.

Beneath the fronds, a game unfolds,
With secrets that the soft earth holds.
From shadowed nooks, the fun will leap,
As every critter stirs from sleep.

So join the frolic, sing along,
In ferny halls where all belong.
For faeries know, with every cheer,
The magic lies in laughter clear!

The Silence of Soft Growth

In the forest where whispers giggle,
Soft patches sprout in a subtle wiggle.
Dance of dew on a lazy morn,
Nature's laughter is never worn.

Fuzzy hats on old grey stones,
Hiding secrets, these tiny thrones.
They laugh as fungi try to play,
While squirrels pause to ponder the day.

Secrets in the Damp Earth

Beneath the soil where shadows drop,
Wiggly worms do a disco bop.
They dig and squirm in muddy blight,
Turning dirt into a veggie delight.

Fungi whisper in cheeky tones,
Sharing tales with the clunky stones.
A root party with no RSVP,
Where every critter is wild and free.

Soft Footfalls on Velvet Sleep

Tiptoe through the bedding trees,
Giggling leaves tease the buzzing bees.
Squirrels scamper, quick as a thought,
In this lush world, joy is caught.

Underfoot, the carpet glows,
As nighttime's laughter gently flows.
The critters party till the dawn,
Where sleepy dreams and giggles spawn.

Nature's Green Embrace

In a blanket of emerald dreams,
Laughter echoes in bubbling streams.
Frogs jump in silly, splashing mess,
Making ripples in their dapper dress.

Leaves chuckle in the morning sun,
As playful shadows have their fun.
Nature's hugs are warm and wide,
With creatures peeking, eyes open wide.

Ferns and Fables Unfolding

In the forest where ferns dance,
A squirrel dropped his lunch by chance,
A sandwich with mustard so bright,
He laughed, 'Not dinner, just a bite!'

Beneath the leaves, a tale is spun,
Of bird debates and squirrel fun,
Who's the fastest? Who's the best?
All while the rabbit takes a rest.

The crow caws loud, the owl snoozes,
In leafy thrones, the critters chooses,
A court of whims, a royal jest,
In tangled roots, they love to rest.

With every leaf, a secret shared,
In laughter, all their worries spared,
Embrace the silly, nature's blend,
Where humor lies, and worries mend.

The Luminescence of Life's Layer

Underneath the glowing light,
Fireflies argue, who's most bright,
They blink and dance, a lively debate,
'A twinkling star, let's celebrate!'

Among the blooms, the ants conspire,
Planning a feast by the moonlight fire,
While grumpy gnomes, with hats so tall,
Bicker over who's the best of all.

A turtle slows, to join the chat,
'Patience, my friends, is where it's at!'
The rabbits giggle at the show,
As daisies bloom all in a row.

In this realm where laughter flows,
And every creature wears a pose,
Life's a game of silly cheer,
Where nature whispers, 'Come and leer!'

Sheltered in the Embrace of Green

Beneath the limbs where shadows play,
A frog tries croaking the blues away,
But every leap makes a funny splash,
As dragonflies zoom, all in a dash.

A turtle's pace, while steady and slow,
Makes the fastest rabbit stop to glow,
'You're winning at life,' the hedgehog quips,
While sipping dew from the morning drips.

The oaks conspire, their leaves all sway,
Whispers of secrets from yesterday,
'Did you hear about the bear who danced?'
The bushes giggle, all entranced.

In every nook, the laughter blends,
A cheerful song as nature sends,
Wrapped in green, where joy is seen,
Life's a romp, a whimsical scene.

Beneath the Sway of Ancient Boughs

Beneath the boughs that twist and weave,
A raccoon waves, 'I can't believe!
I thought that snack would be a breeze,
But all I found were angry bees!'

The woodpecker taps a silly beat,
As rabbits hop and dance on their feet,
'Join us here, let's form a crew,
For every nut, a joke or two!'

With shadows casting funny shapes,
And beetles donning tiny capes,
The forest floor is a stage for play,
Where laughter echoes day by day.

Under the trees, the mischief hums,
A chorus of critters, giggles and drums,
In nature's heart, where fun resides,
Joy spills over where humor hides.

Reveries upon a Living Carpet

On the ground where green clouds lay,
I thought I'd found a spot to play.
But owls and frogs would have a laugh,
As I slipped and fell, my legs a chaff.

I thought that I'd take just a seat,
But life has ways to bring defeat.
A squishy fluff beneath my rear,
Turns to a cushion, oh so queer!

The ants parade, they march along,
While I croon out a silly song.
They roll their eyes, they shake their heads,
Guess I'll stick to my comfy beds.

So next time when I sit and muse,
I'll check for squish before I choose.
My thoughts may be bright, but watch your back,
For nature's prank is quite on track!

The Quietude of Green Thoughts

In shady spots where critters roam,
I ponder if I should go home.
Yet vines and ferns laugh with a grin,
And remind me that fun's about to begin.

With every step, a spongy feel,
Like stepping on a silly meal.
I question if this path is wise,
Or just a plot to catch surprise.

A chipmunk blinks, then gives a shush,
While butterflies perform their hush.
This tranquil space, so full of jest,
Could fool my mind—it's truly blessed.

A thought escapes, it starts to giggle,
Between the leaves, I start to wiggle.
In verdant thoughts, I chase the day,
With nature's jokes to guide my way!

Life's Subtle Reminders

I meander through a fuzzy zone,
Where even rocks have stories shown.
Each step I take, a rubbery prance,
Life reminds me I can't dance.

The grass tickles at my toes,
With every kick, a laugh that grows.
A patch of goo brings forth a cheer,
It's just a leaf—oh dear, oh dear!

Napping gnomes give me a wink,
"Don't jump around, you'll surely sink!"
But still I twirl, with glee and style,
Earning smirks from every isle.

So heed the signs that life decrees,
In each soft squish, hear giggling pleas.
Laughing at my clumsy plight,
I find joy in the slippy light!

Echoes on a Hidden Path

A trail that's soft beneath my feet,
Whispers tales both funny and sweet.
I tiptoe lightly, heart full of fun,
As critters chuckle, "Here she comes!"

The branches sway, they seem to sneer,
Toward my quirk, each lurch and cheer.
With every crunch, I swear I slip,
A green carpet on my happy trip.

The skies above, they laugh and twirl,
Encouraging my playful whirl.
A squirrel joins in, ready to race,
As I stumble, it scurries with grace.

Echoes linger, laughter's sound,
In this wild world where joys abound.
So let me roam, alive and free,
In every misstep, humor's key!

The Secret Life Beneath

Beneath the rocks, they throw a bash,
Tiny critters in a dash.
Hats of leaf and cups of dew,
Dancing while we're stuck in queues.

A party underground, so sly,
With ants that waltz and snails that fly.
Glimmers of fungi light the night,
A glowworm DJ, such a sight!

The worms all squirm in their best dress,
With roots entwined, they truly impress.
When rain comes down, they make a cheer,
Mud pies served on plates of clear.

So next time you walk and scoff,
Give a nod, don't shake it off.
There's laughter where the green does sprout,
In silly burrows, fun's about!

Imprints of a Silent Dance

In the shadows, whispers play,
Footprints left in green ballet.
The bugs execute a grand pirouette,
While spiders weave their silkenette.

Caterpillars munch with glee,
Unaware of the sight they see,
A sugar ant, a stage designed,
With props of leaves, so well aligned.

And when the moon begins to glow,
Little critters start the show.
Fireflies blink, a disco light,
As crickets chirp into the night.

The forest floor, a dance hall bright,
An insect rave, what pure delight.
When dew drops fall, they groove anew,
In silence, laughter, joy, and hue!

Earthbound Dreams

Under stones and in the shade,
Dreams of roots are softly laid.
Caterpillars snore in stacks,
While slugs sneak snacks and plot hijacks.

Worms write letters in the ground,
To old friends, they've tightly bound.
In doodles made of dirt and grime,
They share tales of the passing time.

A dandelion hopes to soar,
With wishes stuck beneath the floor.
Yet there it sits, with dreams to weave,
A laughing flower with tricks up its sleeve.

So when you ponder skies above,
Remember those who dream of love.
In every crevice, laughter streams,
Where dirt and dreams dance in sunbeams.

Verdant Echoes

In the garden, giggles grow,
Plants whisper secrets, soft and low.
A broccoli crowned like a king,
Rules over peas in a jolly fling.

Fallen leaves form a grand parade,
Marching with joy, though slightly frayed.
Tomatoes laugh as they sit tight,
Enjoying the show in morning light.

A gopher hums a happy tune,
As daisies sway, making room.
Butterflies flutter with playful grace,
Drawing smiles on each little face.

So catch the giggles, hear the cheer,
In every patch, nature holds dear.
The echoes of joy in every green,
Life's a comedy, bright and keen!

Tales from the Forgotten Path

I wandered down a path so old,
Where stories of the trees unfold.
A squirrel dressed in a tiny hat,
Told me to watch where I sat!

The stones giggled, a funny lot,
Telling tales of what they forgot.
A rabbit with a monocle grinned,
'You should've seen the race I pinned!'

Through tangled roots and leafy lines,
They started sharing their old designs.
A snail recited a poet's rhyme,
While ants marched perfectly in time!

So here I sit, under their cheer,
Imagining the speeches I hear.
With nature's wit, how it can tease,
Bringing fun with every breeze!

When Greenery Speaks

In whispers soft, the leaves conspire,
They gossip by the old campfire.
A fern claimed that it once could fly,
'Traveling far beyond the sky!'

The grass chuckled with leafy pride,
'I've been a stage for ants to ride.'
A dandelion turned bright orange,
Said, 'Beauty fades, but laughs encourage!'

'My roots reach deeper than you think,'
A stout oak boomed, then stopped to drink.
And as I listened, lost in thought,
I imagined all that they had fought.

With every rustle, laughter cracked,
As nature's humor stalked and tracked.
In this green world, so rich and neat,
Lies fun in every leafy seat!

A Symphony of Subtle Shades

In hues of green, a concert plays,
With crickets chirping soft arrays.
A beetle danced, oh, what a sight!
'This step's the best—hold on tight!'

The violets blushed with mischief bright,
'As flowers, we conspiracy ignite!'
A radish trumpet blared with flair,
'You'll need a jacket, it's cool out there!'

Each color laughed, each shade had fun,
A paintbrush fight had just begun.
And roots of laughter weaved like threads,
While whispers twirled in flower beds!

This garden stage, a merry crowd,
With nature's sounds both bright and loud.
In every corner, joy abounds,
A symphony of giggles sounds!

Nature's Cloak of Contemplation

Beneath a canopy of leafy schemes,
A wise old turtle shared his dreams.
'I ponder life at a slow pace,
The world is but a funny place!'

The stones, they nodded, wise and gray,
'We've watched the critters dance and play.'
A tiny frog jumped in with glee,
'What's wrong with splashing? Come join me!'

As shadows flickered, bright and sly,
A busting bumblebee flew by.
It claimed it knew all there was to see,
But buzzed around like it was free!

In dappled light, these thoughts collide,
While nature wraps us, arms open wide.
In laughter's shade, we'll sit and muse,
Each curious moment, we'll never lose!

Whispers of the Woodland Floor

In the woods where critters play,
Fungi host a grand ballet.
Squirrels dance to rhythm sweet,
While acorns tumble at their feet.

A hedgehog sings a silly tune,
Beneath the light of a silvery moon.
Frogs in bow ties join the fun,
Ribbiting jokes 'til day is done.

Trees giggle and shake their leaves,
As owls roll their eyes at thieves.
Bunnies hop in silly lines,
While chipmunks sip on herbal wines.

With every rustle and light bounce,
The forest shares its funny flounce.
A land of whimsy, wild and free,
Hiding laughter beneath each tree.

Green Dreams Beneath the Canopy

Under the branches, a gnome sleeps tight,
Dreaming of carrots in the soft moonlight.
His hat's on backwards, what a sight!
That silly little dreamer with all his might!

Ladybugs wearing capes take flight,
Joining together for a giggly night.
Beetles debating if they should dance,
While fireflies twinkle - oh, what a chance!

Pitching tents made of leafy green,
A wacky world, a silly scene.
Chasing shadows that play hide and seek,
In this kingdom where the odd is unique.

And now a raccoon, with a hat so grand,
Brushes his paw on a tiny stand.
A game of cards with a wise old crow,
As laughter echoes in the afterglow.

Shadows of the Silent Grove

In shadows deep where squirrels cling,
A cactus costume is all the rage thing.
Badgers picnic with sandwiches fine,
While a wise old owl sips on brine.

The whispers here are soft and quirky,
Where pine cones comment, a bit jerky.
A stroll reveals a patch of wit,
Each step a giggle, every moment a hit.

Beneath the canopy, stories unfold,
Of trees that gossip, both wise and bold.
With snickers and chuckles that never cease,
Nature's humor, a delightful peace.

In this grove, secrets gently swirl,
As twigs share tales in a soft pearl.
Nature's ensemble, a laugh riot,
In shadows deep, there's fun to try it!

Nature's Velvet Tapestry

A tapestry woven with laughter bright,
Each petal and leaf brings pure delight.
Butterflies waltz in a pocket of air,
While ants throw parties without a care.

Rabbits wear glasses, such a sight,
Reading novels by the pale starlight.
And hedgehogs chuckle as they scuttle,
On tiny paths, they laugh and cuddle.

Whimsical vines climb high with flair,
As flowers gossip, sharing their hair.
The breeze tells tales of long-lost glee,
In nature's quilt, there's laughter spree.

In every nook, in every cup,
A celebration for all to sup.
With roots of mirth in the soil found,
Nature's humor spins all around.

Dreams Held in Green Hands

In a patch of green where odd things grow,
A squirrel debates if he's too slow.
He wears a hat made of finest leaves,
And argues with ants about who achieves.

A turtle thinks he's a speedy chap,
But trips on a root during his nap.
An old tree grins, its bark full of charm,
While grass whispers jokes, calm and warm.

Beneath the ferns, a frog sings loud,
Of dreams of flight and being proud.
The dragonflies laugh, buzzing all around,
As gnats dance like they're highly renowned.

All this life in a green embrace,
With giggles and grins, they share the space.
Among the jokes and the quirky bands,
Are the wildest dreams held in green hands.

Reflections in the Underbrush

In the tangled weeds, a mirror's found,
A critter stares with eyes all around.
He tries on a flower as a silly hat,
And wonders if it makes him look fat.

The shadows chuckle, the thickets sway,
As butterflies giggle and flutter away.
A stoat checks his whiskers, gives a bold grin,
Thinking he's dashing in his twiggy skin.

A snail gives guidance, slow and sure,
Says humor's the key to life's grand tour.
As brambles snicker and twigs do tease,
This underbrush holds laughter with ease.

Reflections abound in the chaos here,
Where every bush whispers a cheeky cheer.
In the deep green shade, come take a look,
For silly sights are in every nook.

A Green Veil of Daydreams

Beneath a leafy curtain, dreams trot,
Where beetles debate if they're fancy or not.
A ladybug flaunts her paint-like grace,
While grasshoppers leap in a humorous race.

The sun peeks down, making shadows play,
While bunnies hop with mischief today.
They plan a party with carrots galore,
And giggle as they plot some more lore.

In the gentle breeze, stories float wide,
Of crickets who dance with modesty pride.
With every paw print, the green veil sways,
Sharing secrets and laughs in their own fun ways.

So let's tiptoe softly through this dream,
Where everything's wacky and not quite what it seems.
In a world where laughter and green intertwine,
Every whimsical thought starts to shine.

The Heartbeat of the Hidden

In the shadows, where secrets lie,
A hedgehog scoffs, "Hope I can fly!"
With a wig made of twigs, he puffs with pride,
While beetles buzz by, giggling wide.

The mushrooms hold meetings, chatting away,
Discussing funny things to brighten the day.
With spores sprinkled, the air fills with glee,
As the forest hums its wild symphony.

A raccoon, with mischief and food on his mind,
Sneaks past a picnic, hopes to unwind.
But the sandwiches sigh, "We're not so great,"
As the critters all join in this whimsical fate.

So here in the green, where laughter's akin,
Each heartbeat's a joke, a whimsical din.
In the hidden spaces, life's humor spins,
Of all the chuckles this forest begins.

Embracing the Unseen

In a world of shadows, I trip and roll,
Bumping into dreams, they take their toll.
Invisible giggles, run through the grass,
Making me chuckle as moments pass.

A squirrel with secrets, hides in the bark,
Cracks jokes about humans who park in the dark.
Leaves flutter down like papers in flight,
Whispering sarcasm from morning till night.

I chase after whispers, they giggle and flee,
While pretending to search for my cup of green tea.
Each nook and cranny hides laughter so sweet,
A treasure of humor, at our wandering feet.

So here's to the unseen, the laughter they sow,
In the tangle of branches, where silliness grows.
I raise my tea high to the chuckles disguised,
In this joyful forest, where laughter is prized.

The Breath of Old Trees

Old trees sigh softly, their voices a song,
While they laugh at the people who fumble along.
They plot silly ventures under their crowns,
And chuckle at humans in well-meaning frowns.

A squirrel with spectacles reads from the bark,
Tales of the past while I stumble and spark.
The roots giggle too, they tickle the ground,
With whispers of nonsense that echo around.

Leaves burst with laughter, like ticklish shouts,
As I'm lost in the thicket, surrounded by doubts.
Branches are giggling like old friends at play,
Each rustle a joke they can't help but say.

In the breath of old trees, I find my delight,
With their quirky humor, I laugh in the light.
Next time you wander, be sure to just freeze,
And listen for laughter in the breath of the trees.

Woven Tales of Silence

In the quiet of green, where silence weaves round,
Funny tales linger, and giggles abound.
A snail wearing slippers moves slow as a tease,
While talking to shadows with whimsical ease.

Beneath tangled branches, the whispers unite,
Creating a story both strange and polite.
Charming and quirky, the patterns unfold,
With laughter like sunlight on tapestries old.

The shadows play tag with the flicker of light,
As flowers throw parties that last through the night.
Every heart skipped beat— a punchline in bloom,
Dry leaves tease the wind, humoring the gloom.

So listen closely, my friend, to the breeze,
Where tales spin in silence, with jokes that appease.
The laughter of nature is woven so fine,
In the tapestry of life, it sparkles and shines.

Whispers Among the Roots

Down by the roots, where the secrets are thin,
Funny banter bubbles, sweet chaos within.
A rabbit narrates tales of his trials big,
While snickering beetles dance a comical jig.

The earthworms know gossip, they wriggle and squirm,
With quirky reports that just make you squirm.
They share silly stories from under the ground,
About bumping their heads where no ceilings are found.

In the dark, cool spaces, laughter rolls wide,
The fungi throw shindigs, with laughter as pride.
They poke fun at the toes that step on the grass,
Reminding us all how to chuckle and pass.

So join in the whispers, get low to the earth,
Where the roots hold the secrets and laughter gives birth.
In the depths of their chatter, a joy we can tune,
To the playful perspective of life under moon.

Beneath the Blanket of Life

Beneath the leaves, a squirrel sneezes,
Frogs debate on who's the greasiest.
A worm gets tangled in a shoe lace,
While a snail competes in a slow race.

The grass says "Hey! Be careful, buddy!"
As a hedgehog rolls, feeling quite nutty.
Nature's comedy, we just can't miss,
Flip-flops and plants share a cheeky kiss.

What's that sound, a buzzing delight?
Bees playing tag, what a silly sight!
Flowers gossip in colors so bright,
A dance of petals in morning light.

So, take a seat, let's giggle and roar,
Nature's laughter is hard to ignore.
With each little giggle, life feels more fun,
Beneath the blanket, we're all just one.

Thoughts Entwined in Greenery

The ferns exchange secrets on their tips,
While daisies teach sunflowers to do flips.
Crickets play tunes, the flutes of the night,
I think they're up to something, what a sight!

A ladybug wearing a hat just right,
Happily chatting with mushrooms by night.
Each leaf a whisper, each vine a sigh,
Nature's a joker, oh me, oh my!

A bear in pajamas, yes, it's no jest,
Dreams of honey while taking his rest.
A ticklish breeze steals away a hat,
And here comes a raccoon, looking for that!

With laughter sprouting like wildflowers bright,
Let's cherish these moments, oh what a sight.
In the greenery, silliness reigns, you see,
Nature's a comedian, so wild and free.

The Serenity of Forgotten Paths

On a path where no one ever goes,
A mushroom holds court, with wise words it shows.
A hedgehog, the judge, in a fuzzy old cloak,
As laughter erupts from a wise-cracking oak.

Tangled roots tell tales of days gone by,
Of crickets with dreams and butterflies high.
Lonesome stones giggle with bits of old dust,
Every twist and turn, a must-see, a must.

Bumblebees dance like they own the place,
While a sly fox trots with a charming grace.
Squirrels squabble over acorns, oh dear,
Tripping over twigs with nothing but cheer.

So wander these ways, where whimsy abounds,
Nature's a party with laughter as sounds.
In the forgotten, life wears a grin so wide,
With each cozy path, joy's there to abide.

Hushed by Nature's Hand

In a quiet nook, where shadows play,
Nature whispers secrets in her own way.
A wise old toad croaks a riddle or two,
As butterflies giggle, collecting their due.

The trees tell jokes in the rustling breeze,
While a raccoon tickles a belly with ease.
The brook joins in with its babbling flow,
Giggling and gurgling, it steals the show.

A curtain of leaves hides the scoffing owl,
As crickets host parties on the prowl.
The moonlight chuckles, scattering dreams,
In the stillness, life is bursting at the seams.

So hush for a moment, hear nature's jest,
Beneath her soft cover, we're all her guests.
With each burst of laughter, the day comes alive,
In the heart of the wild, joy seems to thrive.

Timeless Reflections in the Shade

In the park where shadows play,
Squirrels dance, bright leaves sway.
A pigeon walks, all fluff and pride,
It struts around, like a morning guide.

The sun peeks through, with playful glee,
A picnic spread, come join with me.
Ants march on, in their grand parade,
While I debate, should I be afraid?

A sandwich flies, thanks to a breeze,
That clever mouse, with such expertise!
We laugh as crumbs settle like dew,
In this timeless shade where fun feels new.

And as we chat, old tales unfold,
Of past inventions, daring, bold.
In laughter's grip, we find our shade,
Life's silly moments, never fade.

Reveries Wrapped in Nature's Embrace.

Upon the hill where daisies glow,
A rabbit hops, but oh, so slow!
His little tail wags, full of bliss,
Does he know where it is?

Beneath the trees, the critters scheme,
A raccoon dreams of a midnight cream.
He whispers soft to the nearby frog,
Who croaks replies, lost in the fog.

A fox trots by, with a smile too wide,
Poised to tease, filled with pride.
While butterflies burst, in colorful arrays,
They flutter around, in charming displays.

With every giggle that escapes my lips,
Nature's playground makes me flip.
In this embrace with what surrounds,
The funniest tales of life abound.

Emerald Whispers

Green blades chuckle beneath our feet,
While tiny bugs hold a grand meet.
A ladybug rolls, a tiny dare,
To make it home with style and flair.

The brook sings songs of splashes bright,
As frogs join in, what a sight!
They croon their tunes, no shame to show,
For nature's stage, it's quite the show.

Leaves above with secrets tease,
Whispering tales in the gentle breeze.
We stop to listen, laughter erupts,
As squirrels avoid mischief, feeling corrupt.

In this enchanted, leafy domain,
The humor flows like summer rain.
With each giggle, I find my way,
In emerald whispers, I choose to stay.

Beneath the Canopy

Underneath the leafy arch,
A turtle's slow in a leafy march.
While birds croon in a tweet-tweet way,
They make my worries seem far away.

I spy a snail, oh what a sight,
Carrying home, oh what a plight!
He slips and slides, all in a rush,
While nearby flowers softly hush.

Giggles echo from hidden nooks,
As squirrels conspire, planning their brooks.
Their clever tricks, so full of glee,
Nature's jesters, they're wild and free.

In this canopy, fun seems to rise,
A dance of laughter beneath the skies.
With every chuckle, life feels grand,
Here in nature's playful land.

Echoes in the Emerald Underbrush

In the green depths, critters chatter,
A squirrel with style, oh what a clatter!
A rabbit rolled over, found his new game,
While a turtle just laughed, calling them lame.

The fungi are gossiping, sharing their news,
About yesterday's party and who wore the shoes.
A raccoon did salsa, quite out of tune,
Under the watchful glance of the moon.

As shadows grow longer, the stories arise,
From a whispering breeze that tickles the skies.
"Did you hear," says a bug, "that buzzed by a tree?
Its wings were so vibrant, just like me!"

With laughter so hearty, the forest gives cheer,
Each echo a joke, each twig lends an ear.
In these emerald halls where the wild things roam,
Every nook tells a tale, and they all feel like home.

Secrets Beneath the Old Oak

Under the oak, where the shadows play,
A chipmunk declares it's 'Snack Time' today!
With acorns stacked high like a goofy chap,
He slips, takes a tumble, then sets up a map.

The old oak chuckles, its branches sway free,
"Next time, young lad, don't dance with that bee!"
A squirrel near giggles, does a quick flip,
While the ants organize a snack transport trip.

A crow calls out, "Who stole my last fry?"
"Not me," says the worm, with a dubious sigh.
They make up tall tales of feats and of blunders,
While the oak rolls its rings, and gracefully wonders.

All tales in the hush, of this green, lively place,
From secretive critters that share their sweet grace.
Each whisper, each giggle, a friendship to find,
In the mysteries woven by nature's own mind.

The Soft Embrace of Time

Time gently drapes like a comfy old shawl,
As the toads croak out a whimsical call.
A snail takes its time, and oh what a scene,
Counting the clouds like a methodical machine.

The sun yawns and stretches, peeking through leaves,
While a beetle complains, "I'm late for my peaves!"
A dance of the dandelions sways in the breeze,
While a chipmunk just shrugs, "I'll nap if you please."

Along comes a hedgehog, fashionably slow,
Sporting a hat made of dew, what a show!
The flowers all giggle, their petals a-flutter,
In the soft embrace, rumors start to utter.

Time's playful patter, a tick-tock of cheer,
As life rolls on by, we gather to hear.
In this cozy old nook where everyone shines,
The days waltz along, writ in twisty designs.

Petals and Ponderings

With petals in hand, let's ponder a bit,
What happens to shoes that fit but don't fit?
A bee buzzes loudly, yelling, "All mine!"
While a flower just blushes, "Can't you read the sign?"

A ladybug jokes, "I'm the star of the show,
Twirling and spinning, come watch me glow!"
The daisies all giggle, they know the real score,
It's the snail with the charm that brings everyone more.

In the garden at dusk, mysteries bubble,
As a worm tells a story of digging through trouble.
The moon winks down, soaking in all the fun,
While frogs leap around, thinking they're number one.

So here among petals, on this whimsical spree,
We slip into dreams, oh so silly and free.
With laughter and secrets, the night whispers low,
In the sweet blooming garden, where friendships just grow.

The Gentle Pull of the Earth

In the park, I sit and frown,
The grass below, a vibrant gown.
It whispers softly, calls my name,
Yet my shoes won't let me, what a shame!

I tried to leap, felt quite the fool,
The grass just giggled, it's way too cool.
Instead, I chuckled, thought I'd spy,
On worms below that wriggle and lie.

The ground insists, 'You shall remain!'
I asked the tree to share my pain.
It just stood tall, barked with delight,
'You're stuck with me, so lose the fight!'

So here I am, held by the Earth,
As grass plays jokes, oh what mirth!
Next time I'll bring a secret plan,
To outsmart the ground, or at least, a fan!

When Time Stands Still

Clock ticks slow as I sit here,
The flowers nod, both far and near.
I ponder hard, but what's the rush?
A turtle nearby gives a gentle hush.

I blink my eyes, oh there's the sun!
Did it sleep in? Oh, what fun!
I've lost my place in time, alas!
The squirrels laugh, as they quickly pass.

The shadows stretch, begin to play,
In this strange game, it's a funny day.
I'm stuck on a bench with thoughts awry,
'Get up!' they tease, but I'm shy, oh my!

Time decides to rest its case,
While I giggle in this lovely place.
So I'll recline, and let them jest,
In this peculiar time, I'm truly blessed!

A Dialogue with the Earth

I spoke to the soil, thought I'd chat,
It grumbled back, 'You, silly brat!'
I asked about roots and what they crave,
It whispered, 'Less talk, more digging, be brave!'

I told it jokes, about the rain,
It rolled its eyes, 'Please, not again!'
The worms all giggled, but held their ground,
I laughed so hard, I almost drowned!

A rock chimed in, 'You're quite a clown,'
I took a bow, gave it a frown.
'You'll never guess my hidden skill,'
I said, with glee, 'I dig for thrills!'

We all had fun, this earthy crew,
Conversations where laughter grew.
The leaves would sway, and oh, what cheer,
In this funny chat, I shed a tear!

The Sigh of Old Stones

The stones all sit so still and grey,
They breathe a sigh, it's been a day.
'We've seen it all,' they start to share,
'From shoes to ghosts, we've faced the scare!'

'Oh, but do tell!' I urged in glee,
'Of all the things, what's fun' I plea.
'We've seen the world spin round and round,
But miss the laughs, by leaps and bounds!'

They rolled their eyes, each crack with sass,
'We'd join the fun, but we're too crass.'
I offered jokes, they shook with mirth,
'You're quite the jester, for what it's worth!'

Then came a breeze, oh what a tease,
The stones just chuckled, swaying with ease.
'Life's not all woes, but laughter and cheer,
Dear friend, we may be falling, but we're far from drear!'

The Softness of Green Dreams

Underneath the leafy bed,
A frog pops up and then misread,
He leaps with glee, but oh dear me,
He lands right on a bumblebee!

A snail, so slow, shimmies near,
Singing songs no one can hear,
With every inch he does explore,
He finds a pizza slice galore!

Mushrooms dance in silly pairs,
Whispering secrets, while none cares,
They chuckle softly, share a laugh,
At the squirrel who steals their path!

In this realm of leafy chill,
Every creature feels the thrill,
While humans stroll with frowns and fright,
The critters giggle, feeling right!

Twilight Beneath the Canopy

As shadows stretch and twilight calls,
A rabbit trips, then daintily falls,
He shakes it off, with tiny pride,
Racing on, he won't abide!

Before the glow of fireflies,
A raccoon plans his grand disguise,
With mask and hat, he sneaks about,
Swiping snacks without a doubt!

The owls giggle, perched on high,
Watching antics of passerby,
They hoot and tease, it's quite the show,
While moles dig holes beneath the glow!

Magical moments, full of cheer,
In this twilight, all draw near,
Where laughter lingers, tales unfold,
As nature's jesters, brave and bold.

Glimmers of Life's Palette

In the dappled light so fine,
A ladybug drinks herbal wine,
Upside down, she sways with glee,
But spills the drink—oh, classy bee!

A butterfly, with wings of flair,
Sips nectar in the fragrant air,
He sneezes loud, what a surprise,
And wakes the snoozing ladyflies!

Colors swirl like paints on ground,
Each blending in a dance profound,
Yet ants march on, all in a line,
One drops a crumb, causing the shine!

Every hue holds laughter's spark,
Where nature plays, never stark,
With splashes of joy as brush and glee,
Life's canvas blooms, so wild and free!

In the Shade of Still Thoughts

Beneath the trees where whispers blend,
A rabbit hops, makes no amend,
He pauses, ponders life and fate,
Then trips again—oh dear, too late!

A butterfly thinks she's quite grand,
In a sunbeam, she takes a stand,
But the wind gives her a little shove,
And down she flops, not quite in love!

Squirrels gather, plotting schemes,
While planning out their daydreams,
They toss acorns—what a hit!
One lands right on a sleeping pit!

In this realm where thoughts collide,
All creatures laugh and take the ride,
Life rolls on, both wild and sweet,
In the shade, with feeling discreet!

A Tapestry of Ferns

In the forest, ferns dance around,
Waving like they've lost their found.
They tickle the toes of the unwary,
Who stumble upon the quite contrary.

A squirrel spies them, eyes narrowing wide,
Plots a heist, where secrets abide.
With acorns in tow, he takes to the air,
While the ferns giggle, 'It's not really fair!'

Ferny whispers in the wind take flight,
As shadows frolic, dodging the light.
'Life's a joke,' they chortle and scream,
In this leafy world, nothing's as it seems.

So come hear the tales the ferns intertwine,
Where laughter is rich, and the sun is divine.
In this greenery, all worries subside,
As nature's punchlines will surely provide.

Echoes of the Untamed

In the wild, where the echoes rove,
A witty coyote tries to 'improve.'
He howls jokes to the amusing moon,
'What's a wolf to do? Just howl a tune!'

Chirpy crickets join the gag,
With little legs, they tap and brag.
'We're the band, you'd better not fuss!'
While frogs croak, 'It's quite a plus!'

In the underbrush, a bear chuckles low,
'Wanna hear a pun? I really won't go!'
He snickers at ants, so busy and spry,
'You call that teamwork? What a silly pie!'

The night air dances with glee and gags,
Amidst the trees, where the laughter brags.
So roam wild, forget all your woes,
For humor blossoms where untamed life grows.

Enchanted Trails

Along the trails where starlight peeks,
A raccoon jests, 'What's up with leaks?'
'Don't ask me, I just found some pails!'
'You'd think I'm wet, but I just tell tales!'

A fawn prances with drapes so bright,
'Is this my dress or a strange bird's flight?'
As laughter echoes through leafy vibes,
'Let's strut our stuff, no need for bribes!'

The wind tickles and frolics through trees,
While squirrels scamper with endless tease.
'What's green and has whiskers?' they call with glee,
'A salad that's shady, come humor me!'

With overgrown laughs and jumbled lines,
Life unwinds in these quirky shrines.
So wander the trails and join in the cheer,
For every absurdity, it's okay to veer.

The Lure of Life's Patina

Old stones grin under layers of green,
Each crack a story, each crevice unseen.
'What's your secret?' whispers the breeze,
They giggle and say, 'Just age with ease!'

The dandelions buffet at the gates,
'We're weeds with ambitions, not just old mates!'
Their fluffy tops sway, caught in the jest,
As daffodils yell, 'At least we're the best!'

A snail with swagger, he slugs on by,
'Hurry? Please, I don't even try!'
While pollen drifts in an awkward spin,
'Life's a slow dance, now let's begin!'

So treasure the odd, the quaint and bizarre,
Under the patina of life's shining star.
For every chuckle and every last tease,
We're all just here, doing what we please.

Shaded Memories of the Forest

In the forest where squirrels croon,
A raccoon dancing under the moon.
With acorns wearing tiny hats,
And owls sharing jokes with chubby bats.

Fungi with flair, they strut in line,
While chipmunks laugh over some old wine.
Trees whisper secrets, none can decode,
As I trip over roots on this leafy road.

Berries are flinging their juicy mess,
The deer look back, quite unimpressed.
A stream giggles, splashes like a child,
In this silly wild, where joy's compiled.

So here's to tales of woodland delights,
Where laughter's woven in the nights.
In nature's party, I'm a glad guest,
Among all the quirks, I feel so blessed!

Lush Lullabies of the Landscape

In meadows bright where daisies sing,
A grasshopper dons a tiny bling.
Butterflies float as if on a quest,
Laughing at rabbits who won't take a rest.

The sun tickles the cheeks of the ants,
While frogs in their hats do a dance.
Breezes giggle through the tall green grass,
As daisies whisper, 'please let us pass!'

The clouds tell tales, drifting and slow,
While ladybugs wave to the crows below.
Each blade of grass has a joke to tell,
In this happy place, all is quite swell.

So let's stroll through this cartoonish land,
Where nature stretches out a big hand.
In every nook, a chuckle to find,
With laughter and bliss, perfectly aligned!

Dreams in a Green Embrace

Amidst the ferns, a snail takes a ride,
On a little leaf, feeling quite wide.
He shouts, 'Look at me! I'm flying at last!'
As raindrops giggle, they fall from the past.

Toadstools wear vests, oh what a sight!
While insects break out for a dance party night.
A worm plays bass with a leaf as a drum,
While crickets come in, all fuzzy and numb.

Fireflies twinkle, like stars in the gloom,
As insects gather in a leafy room.
They toast their juice and cheer every toast,
For nature's funny and quirky host.

In this green embrace, where laughter is free,
Find joy in the quirks of this leafy spree.
With starlit wishes and dreams that trace,
Giggles abound in this merry place!

The Poetry of Fern and Stone

Under rocks, the wise old tales live,
As the ferns chuckle and dance to forgive.
A tortoise reads from its favorite tome,
While crickets clap as they call it home.

Stones tell stories of time gone by,
While dandelions puff as they sigh.
The shadows prance, in playful delight,
As squirrels argue over a nutty bite.

A woodpecker drums like there's no tomorrow,
While flowers gossip, exchanging sorrow.
In this bumpy world where laughter roams,
Even the rocks have had their poems.

So let's celebrate with each twist and turn,
In nature's laughter, there's so much to learn.
For amidst ferns and stones, a jest does linger,
In this wild comedy, life's an eager singer.

Twilight's Soft Embrace

In the twilight, shadows play,
Gnomes and elves dance away,
Pinecones giggle, toadstools cheer,
Who knew forest life had so much beer?

Fungi hold a raucous feast,
Fairies bring the bubbly yeast,
Under the stars, their laughter rings,
Nature's party, oh what joy it brings!

Inside the bark, secrets hide,
Squirrels plotting their next slide,
Trees whisper tales of minor crime,
Who knew the woods had so much lime?

With a splash, a critter falls,
Echoes of their silly calls,
Twilight wraps them in a hug,
Nature's joy, nothing to shrug!

Beneath the Whispering Growth

In the thicket, giggles swell,
A rabbit's joke, a turtle's yell,
Laughter flows like rivers wide,
While bushes share a laugh inside.

Beneath the leaves, a cabaret,
Worms in tuxedos sway and play,
Grasshoppers tap their tiny feet,
Enticing ants to join the beat.

The dandelion, proud and tall,
Tells knock-knock jokes, keeping all,
While daisies roll in fits of glee,
"Who knew plants could be so free?"

Caterpillars sing of dreams,
Floating on their leafy beams,
Nature's humor, wild and fun,
In the green, we all are one!

Hidden Thoughts in a Leafy Nest

A hidden laugh in every leaf,
Nature's whispers, oh so brief,
Squirrels plotting a nutty deal,
Beneath the boughs, they squeal and squeal.

The grass peeks up, for a peek show,
As snails take their time, moving slow,
With every glimmering ray of sun,
They plot new ways to have more fun!

Chirping crickets, a band of sorts,
Performing shows in leafy courts,
While woodpeckers add a beat,
Nature's symphony, oh so sweet!

In shadows where the wild things dwell,
They share their secrets, all too well,
"Ever heard the one about the tree?"
It cracked up so hard, a sight to see!

The Subtle Elegance of Growth

Layers of laughter, softly told,
Nature's jesters, young and old,
Buds pop up with cheerful grins,
While beetles flaunt their shiny skins.

A shy sprout peeks from the ground,
Feeling brave when friends abound,
"Watch me dance!" it shouts with glee,
While nearby leaves shake wild and free!

Mushrooms bow in playful sways,
As if to steal the sun's bright rays,
Each petal flaunts its colored dress,
Nature's ball, with such finesse!

Here in the garden, humor flows,
Every blade of grass knows the shows,
As laughter rises, so do we,
In nature's realm, wild and free!

Silence Wrapped in Softness

In the woods where whispers dwell,
A frog croaks like a tolling bell.
Squirrels gossip on the ground,
In this quiet, humor's found.

Beneath the trees, the shadows dance,
A beetle takes a clumsy chance.
With each slip, the laughter grows,
Nature's jesters in their shows.

A sloth's yawn, a turtle's sigh,
Laughter bubbles as they lie.
Snails pull pranks with slimy flair,
In this soft laughter, we share.

So let us chuckle, soft and light,
In the woods, everything's right.
With every rustle, nature's tease,
We find the joy in gentle breeze.

Enchanted by the Earth's Embrace

A wandering worm tells tales of plight,
As a raccoon tries to steal a bite.
The hedgehog giggles, round and prickly,
While ants march home quite slickly.

Underneath the ancient tree,
A spider spins with wild glee.
Caught in webs, the breeze is tight,
Looks like dinner is in sight!

Frogs wear crowns of dewdrop beads,
While squirrels plot their daring deeds.
With sunlight glinting through the leaves,
Nature's laughter softly weaves.

Oh, to frolic without care,
With every critter always there.
Enchanted realms beneath our feet,
In this kingdom, joy's complete.

Reflection in a Verdant Veil

In the garden, giggles sprout,
As flowers bloom and chase about.
Bees wear hats of fuzzy fluff,
While blossoms argue, 'Who's enough?'

A rabbit hops with style and grace,
Count the carrots in the race!
Chasing shadows in the sun,
In this verdant world, we run.

Leaves are whispers, giggles shared,
Among the ferns, all is bared.
A snail's pace is like a slow ballet,
Every move a funny display.

With laughter rippling through the air,
Life's little moments without a care.
Reflection blooms in every hue,
In this green laughter, we renew.

Beneath the Canopy of Ages

A chattering chipmunk climbs so high,
While leaves exchange a playful sigh.
Beneath the trees, a wise old owl,
Mocks the fox with a cheeky growl.

Crickets serenade the night,
With rhythms that feel just right.
Fireflies waltz in shimmering trails,
Telling secrets with their sails.

Raccoons will scheme and plot all day,
While the sun dips low and fades away.
In this wonder, laughter sings,
As nature dons her joyful wings.

So let us wander, let us play,
In this forest of bright array.
Beneath the ages, spirits soar,
In laughter's arms, forevermore.

Original title:
The Meaning of Life, According to Your Mother

Copyright © 2025 Creative Arts Management OÜ
All rights reserved.

Author: Colin Leclair
ISBN HARDBACK: 978-1-80566-043-9
ISBN PAPERBACK: 978-1-80566-338-6

Horizons of Hope

In the kitchen, the pot's on the boil,
Mom says laughter is the ultimate toil.
With a wink and a smile, she spins a yarn,
"Life's like a dance; don't forget to charn!"

Chasing dreams while wearing mismatched socks,
She juggles the laundry, tickles the clocks.
"If you trip on your toes, just get up and prance,
Life's but a joke; just give it a chance!"

In the backyard, we plant hopes in the ground,
Mom whispers secrets, funny and sound.
"Dig deep for the nuggets that make you smile,
Life isn't a race; enjoy every mile!"

With cookies and stories, she conquers the night,
Mom's unwavering love, my guiding light.
"So toast to the chaos, to laughter in strife,
Tomorrow's a mystery; let's savor this life!"

www.ingramcontent.com/pod-product-compliance
Lightning Source LLC
Chambersburg PA
CBHW071818160426
43209CB00003B/130